Originally published in Dutch by Uitgeverij Snor
© 2012 Uitgeverij Snor
All rights reserved
Published in English by Who's There LLC
Venice, CA 90291
knockknockstuff.com

Edited translation © 2015 Who's There LLC
All rights reserved
Knock Knock is a trademark of Who's There LLC
Made in China

The rights to this book have been negotiated by the
literary agency Sea of Stories, www.seaofstories.com

Concept by Uitgeverij Snor
Original text by Elsbeth Teeling in collaboration
with Gerard Janssen
Design and artwork by Studio Pomp

ISBN: 978-160106666-4
UPC: 82570350042-4

10 9 8 7 6 5 4 3 2 1

# 99 PICK-ME-UPS FOR NEW MAMAS

How to relax, survive, and even enjoy those first few months!

KNOCK KNOCK®

VENICE, CALIFORNIA

# PREFACE

Everyone knows that your life changes when you become a mother. Plenty of people all around will tell you so. When I was pregnant the first time, people constantly told me, "Better enjoy it while you can." I just let them have their say, 'cause I had no clue.

And then, wham—all of a sudden, I was a mother. Part of an entire new club. And gradually I turned into a walking cliché. I started singing weird songs in the swimming pool (but only when the baby was with me). I took up knitting, showed pictures of my baby to everybody, wore clothes with dried spit-up on them, and . . . lost myself in the process.

Motherhood has many incredible, beautiful, sweet, frustrating, annoying, funny, and hard aspects (quite a few of that last category). The ability to put things in perspective comes in handy if you want to survive. Sometimes, you have to break free from motherhood—if only to remember for a moment that you are more than just a mom. Of course, that can be difficult after weeks without sleep.

That's why this little book was made: to offer support to other mothers in the struggle between their Inner Happy-Go-Lucky Gal and Worrywart Mom. That struggle may be a little different for all of us, but it's basically the same.

This book is not about right or wrong. It's not about how you should care for your baby, or what the baby should eat. This book is about you and me: about the emotions of motherhood that are sometimes hard to explain, and hard to bear, but understood by all mothers. You don't have to be perfect. Relax, Mama!

—Elsbeth Teeling

**WARNING:
DO NOT READ IF YOU'RE
NOT A MOM YET!**

# 1

*Stuff to help you at the beginning*

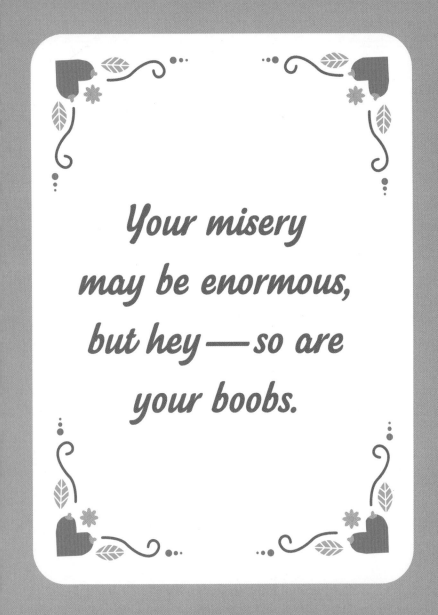

Your misery
may be enormous,
but hey—so are
your boobs.

# YOU'RE ALREADY A SUPERMOM.

You just are.

IT MAY TAKE A WHILE,
BUT EVERYTHING REALLY WILL BE FINE.

## BE SURE TO SHARE
## ALL THE GROSS, PAINFUL
## DETAILS OF YOUR DELIVERY.

It's good for your soul.

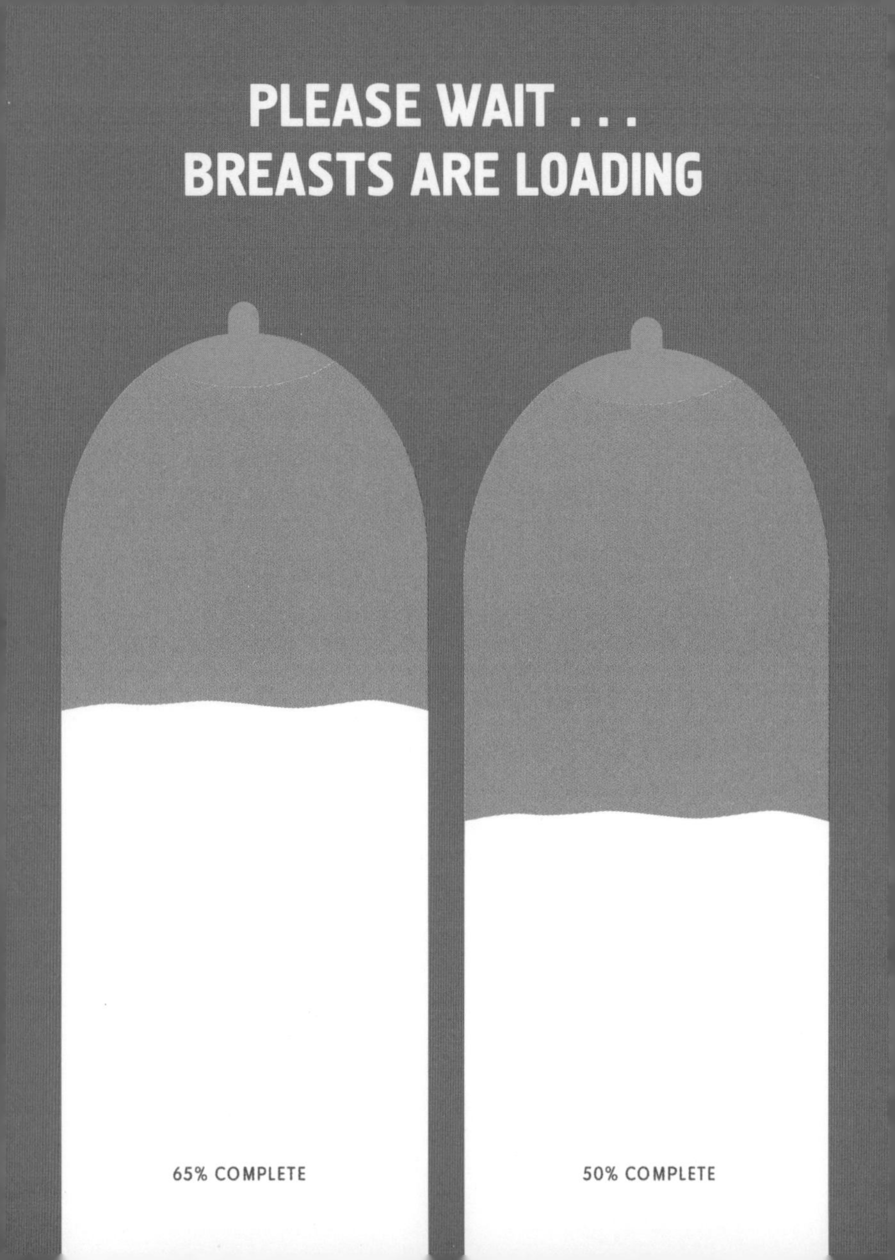
PLEASE WAIT . . .
BREASTS ARE LOADING
65% COMPLETE
50% COMPLETE

**WE APOLOGIZE, BUT CLOUD 9
IS TEMPORARILY OUT OF SERVICE.**

FROM NOW ON, YOUR PUSH-UP BRA
IS YOUR BEST FRIEND.

# IT'S OKAY TO CRY LIKE A NEWBORN BABY.*

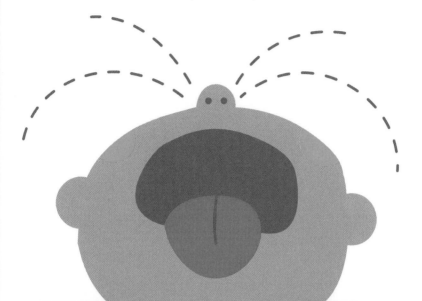

Your body is working hard to return to normal. A lot is going on with your hormones: estrogen is decreasing, prolactin is increasing, and the enzyme monoamine oxidase A is surging, which in turn lowers your levels of serotonin, dopamine, and norepinephrine. This makes you unstable and can give you the feeling, after a day or three, that you're no good as a mom. Any little remark can make you cry.

*And it's okay if this entire page gets soaking wet.

# WORKSHOP #1: DARK CIRCLES

Potatoes contain the enzyme catecholase, which is said to be a skin lightener. Just don't let the potato juice get in your eyes! (Note: some people combine potatoes with grated cucumbers.)

Grate a potato.

Collect the gratings.

Place them on your bags for 15 to 20 minutes.

Wash your face and you'll be glowing again!

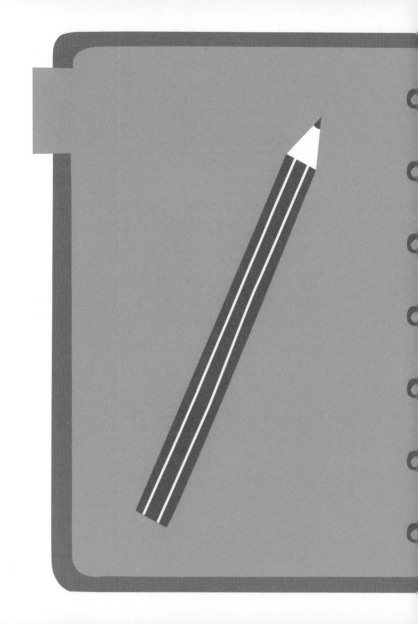

## DON'T TRY TO DO ANYTHING.

Oftentimes, you won't be able to get anything done with a baby in the house.

So don't plan anything, and then every little thing you accomplish will be a bonus.

NOTHING

NADA

ZIP

ZERO

# PLAN
## LIBERALLY.

PACK BAG

BABY POOPS UP
BACKSIDE OF ONESIE

BABY INCONSOLABLE

CLEAN,
CHANGE BABY

RE-DRESS BABY

HUNT FOR PACIFIER;
RE-PACK BAG

MOTHER-IN-LAW
CALLS

BABY THROWS UP
ON CLEAN ONESIE

RE-RE-DRESS BABY;
BABY STILL CRYING

BOOBS BURSTING;
NURSE

PUT BABY IN
CAR SEAT

HUNT FOR CAR KEYS

# DON'T WALK THE WALK
# IF YOU CAN'T TALK THE TALK

LETDOWN

COLIC

MECONIUM

BURP CLOTH

ENGORGEMENT

NURSING PAD

DEVELOPMENTAL
MILESTONE

PLUGGED DUCT

PREGNANCY
DEMENTIA

# FORGET EVERYTHING YOU THINK YOU KNOW ABOUT GOOD MOTHERS.

**PREGNANCY CALENDAR**

# 547 DAYS

= 18 MONTHS = 1.5 YEARS

Is how long it takes, on average, before a woman starts to feel "like a woman" (i.e., sexy, normal, herself) after giving birth. Nine months in and nine months out is a fairy tale. So give yourself a break, Mama!

SLEE

IS

NEW

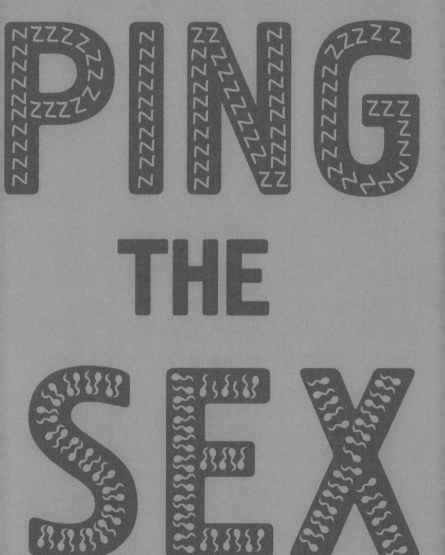

# GIVE IN.

Let it all hang out.

# THE OTHER MOMS ARE ALL JUST WINGING IT, TOO.

# 2

*Stuff to reassure you*

# THINGS YOU SHOULDN'T FEEL GUILTY ABOUT:

You put your baby in his swing when you want to do something for yourself, you don't have time for your husband, you give your baby food from a jar instead of fresh homemade organic puree, your baby can pick up on your stress, you couldn't find a babysitter when your friend had a birthday party, your baby sat in a dirty diaper, your baby goes to daycare, you don't have enough time for him/her, you're happy your baby is asleep, you don't feel like having sex, you don't spend enough time with your girlfriends, you don't use cloth diapers, you're having takeout again, you're not teaching your baby to self-soothe properly, the house is still a mess even though you've been home all day, you'd rather be at home than at a bar with friends, you haven't lost the baby weight, you can't focus at work, you're earning less now, you haven't called your parents in ages, you're spoiling your child, you haven't replied to an email from an old friend, you sometimes miss the pre-baby era, you don't like doing crafts, you can't seem to get dinner ready by six o'clock, you yelled at your child, you weren't consistent, you were late to daycare, you called your husband by the baby's name, you called the baby by the dog's name, you forgot the parent-teacher conference, you're always late to work (and leave early), you haven't started a college fund, you've made your kid a cheese addict at a very young age, you give in too easily, your kid is too loud, you ate the entire bag of candy, your child isn't getting enough nature, you've gossiped about other moms, you didn't go to the gym, your kid is wearing stained clothing, you aren't eating enough fruit and veggies, you talk too much about yourself or your child, you don't pet your dog or cat enough, your kid got diaper rash (again), you didn't send thank-you cards for your child's birthday gifts, you let the dishes pile up, the baby scratched his face/ear, your mom got her Mother's Day card late, you killed a spider and her nest, you didn't take out the trash, the car seat cover smells like a homeless person, you're not keeping up with the news, the baby's bedding isn't organic, you feel guilty all the time.

**SOMETIMES MAMA NEEDS A BOTTLE, TOO.**

# OCCASIONALLY A LITTLE BRIBERY IS OKAY.

- ☑ You're on a plane with a screaming toddler
- ☑ You're tired and nothing else works
- ☑ You're on the phone with your oldest friend
- ☑ Your kid is throwing a tantrum in the supermarket

Mommy
is
mean

## COMPLETE THE FOLLOWING:

### URGENT

SHAVE LEGS.............................

PEDICURE...............................

WRINKLE CREAM.......................

LUXURY CHOCOLATE................

.............................................

.............................................

.............................................

.............................................

.............................................

.............................................

.............................................

.............................................

.............................................

.............................................

.............................................

.............................................

.............................................

.............................................

.............................................

.............................................

.............................................

### NOT URGENT

NEW COUCH............................

DO DISHES..............................

SIGN UP FOR BOOT CAMP.......

GO TO DENTIST.......................

.............................................

.............................................

.............................................

.............................................

.............................................

.............................................

.............................................

.............................................

.............................................

.............................................

.............................................

.............................................

.............................................

.............................................

.............................................

.............................................

.............................................

**TO DO OR NOT TO DO?**

# YOU'RE NOT THE ONLY MOM WHO HAS . . .

yelled
"no yelling!"

let her baby cry because the
monitor wasn't working

brought her kid to daycare
when he was sick

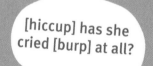

[hiccup] has she
cried [burp] at all?

come home tipsy
to the new babysitter

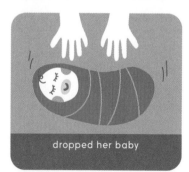

dropped her baby

given herself worry lines

YOU CAN'T SAVE TIME.

## CHECK OFF EVERYTHING THAT APPLIES. YOU:

**Test!**

- [ ] sometimes say, "wow, time flies!"
- [ ] smell bottoms in public
- [ ] are chronically tired (but ignore it)
- [ ] have changed your husband's name to "daddy"
- [ ] say "mommy is going to . . ." instead of "I'm going to . . ."
- [ ] say "potty" instead of "bathroom"
- [ ] say "binky" instead of "pacifier"
- [ ] share as many pictures on social media as possible
- [ ] adjust your boobs in public
- [ ] want to eat your baby
- [ ] pick other people's boogers
- [ ] clean pacifiers by putting them in your mouth
- [ ] find that your biceps are the only part of your body in semi-decent shape
- [ ] basically wear pajamas all the time
- [ ] are convinced that everybody adores your child
- [ ] use diminutives far too often
- [ ] like the smell of your baby's poop

IF YOU DO ANY—OR ALL—OF THESE, IT'S OKAY.
YOU'RE NOT THE ONLY ONE.

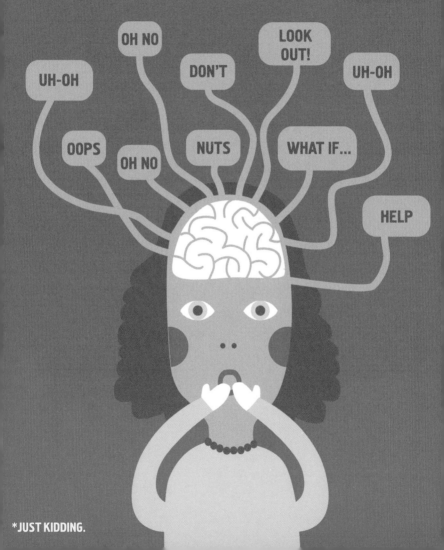

# East or west, baby cries at home best.

*(or when you're shopping)*

Your child will not remember
that you did a great job cleaning the floor.

YES, IT WOULD MAKE GREAT ORGANIC FERTILIZER. BUT YOU'RE WAY TOO BUSY RIGHT NOW FOR GARDENING.

# MOTHERS WHO STAY HOME ARE RIGHT.

# MOTHERS WHO GO TO WORK ARE RIGHT.

**BE CONFIDENT.**

Your child will grow up no matter what,
thanks to you—and sometimes in spite of you.

MOMMY

EASE INTO YOUR NEW ROLE AS A MOTHER.

Many stars in the sky are actually galaxies with trillions of stars in them. So relax. In the big picture, your poochy tummy/ crappy used stroller/chronic tardiness are minor matters.

# 3

*Stuff to help you survive*

# IGNORE WELL-MEANING ADVICE

## Vow of Silence

I solemnly swear never (and absolutely never) to give advice on all the benefits or down-sides of breastfeeding, home births, organic food, or sleep methods to mothers who did not ask for my opinion.

**IT'S NONE OF MY BUSINESS.**

Name: ................................................. Date: ..................

Signature: ....................................................

*Official*

Creating a child
is a miracle;
having a child
is a hassle.

**GRAB A BEER AND GET ON THE DANCE FLOOR!**

You've got more booty to shake!

# TAKE EVERYTHING AS A COMPLIMENT.

IF OTHER PEOPLE TRY TO CRITICIZE YOUR LITTLE ONE (WHICH THEY SHOULD NEVER, EVER DO), PUT A POSITIVE SPIN ON IT:

"That kid is hyperactive." → "They say that's normal for children with gifted parents."

"Wow, he's pretty bossy." → "Yes, he's just like his grandpa—before he became a multimillionaire."

"She's a bit introverted, isn't she?" → "She's already written a book."

"Is he always such a picky eater?" → "He was weaned on gourmet cuisine."

"He's not walking yet?" → "Some people believe that happens with super-intelligent children."

# PUT ON A SMILE EVERY DAY.

When you smile, hundreds of muscles in your face and body relax. Your mood improves, and you can take more on. Smile at a dirty diaper, smile when you're doing the laundry, and smile when you're almost late for daycare.

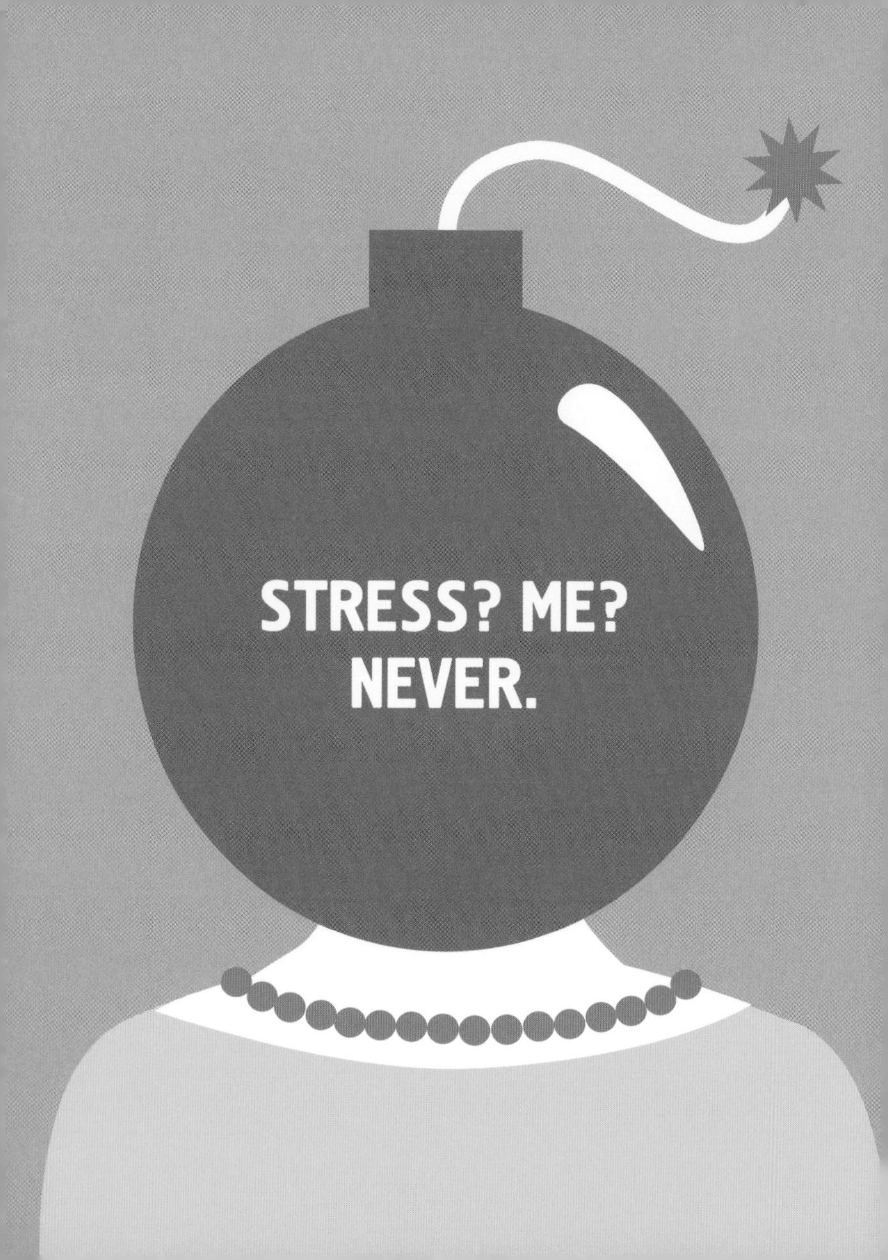
STRESS? ME?
NEVER.

IT MAY TAKE A WHILE BEFORE YOU'RE BACK TO YOUR OLD SELF. YOU'RE BUSY BECOMING YOUR NEW SELF.

# TO-DO LIST:

..................................................

1. Tear out this page and throw it away.

DON'T DO ANYTHING ELSE IN THE MEANTIME.
JUST SIT AND READ THIS BOOK.

# IT REALLY DOES TAKE A VILLAGE TO RAISE A CHILD.

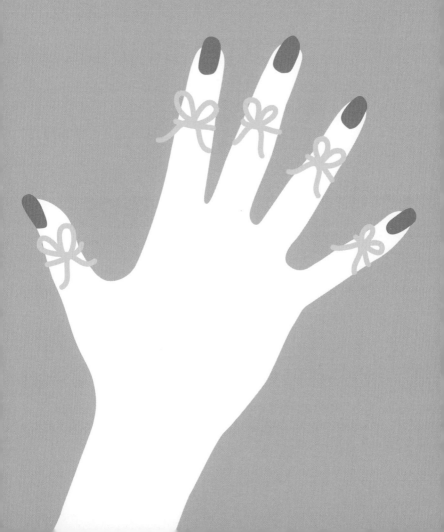

**IF YOU FORGOT IT, IT PROBABLY WASN'T IMPORTANT ANYWAY.**

| | |
|---|---|
| **HYPER MOMMY** | 👎 |
| **TURBO MOMMY** | 👎 |
| **ULTRA MOMMY** | 👎 |
| **TOP MOMMY** | 👎 |
| **SUPER MOMMY** | 👎 |
| **MOMMY** | 👍 |

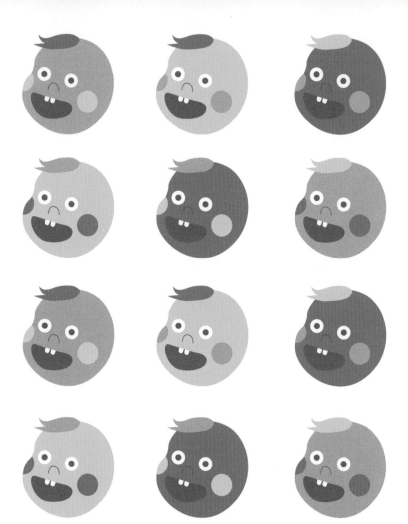

**JUST PRETEND THIS IS YOUR TWELFTH KID.
IT'LL MAKE THINGS MUCH EASIER.**

OPEN A WINDOW.

Oxygen works miracles.

# ANIMALS I HAVE FELT LIKE SINCE GETTING PREGNANT: A CHART

BEACHED WHALE

HUMMINGBIRD LAYING AN OSTRICH EGG

KANGAROO

DAIRY COW

HERMIT CRAB

PACK MULE

MONTH    1    2    3    4    5    6    7    8

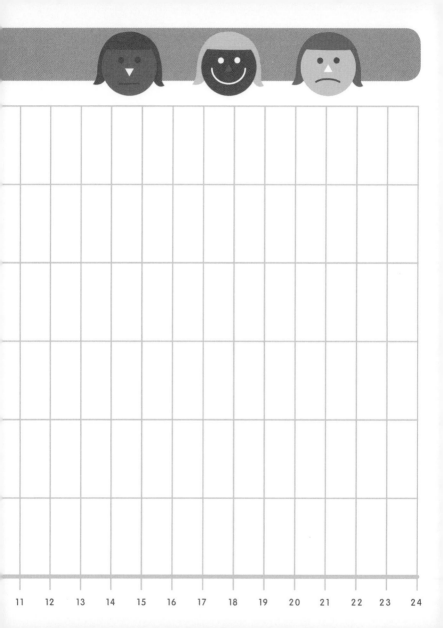

11   12   13   14   15   16   17   18   19   20   21   22   23   24

**TAKE YOUR LONG NIGHTS SERIOUSLY.
LACK OF SLEEP IS DEADLY.**

Feeling unstable? Forgetting things hundreds of times a day?
Go to sleep. Power naps are not called power naps for nothing.
Your brain really does need sleep to set everything right.

**STOP COMPARING YOURSELF!**

# THINGS THAT MAKE MOTHERHOOD LESS FUN:

COMPARING YOURSELF TO MOTHERS WHO BAKE THEIR OWN CAKES, HAVE PERFECT HUSBANDS, AND AMAZING JOBS

SACRIFICING YOURSELF FOR YOUR PARTNER OR YOUR KID

GETTING FRUSTRATED BY UNREALISTIC GOALS (SUCH AS A CLEAN KITCHEN FLOOR)

FEELING GUILTY WHEN YOU TAKE TIME AND SPACE FOR YOURSELF

**MOMMY'S ON STRIKE.**

*Stuff to make you happy*

MAKE YOUR TRASH CAN A TARGET.

It's great to score, especially with diapers.

**I LIKE:**
**BORING FACEBOOK UPDATES**
**FROM PEOPLE WHO DON'T**
**HAVE LIVES EITHER**

**BUY SOMETHING NICE FOR EVERYONE WHO HAS HELPED YOU IN THE LAST FEW MONTHS.**

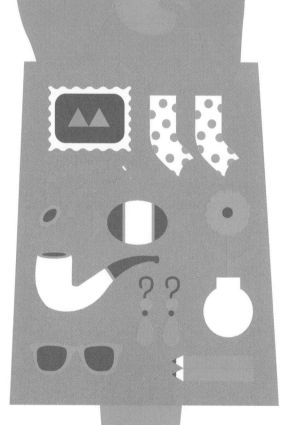

Nobody comes to mind? Start asking for help more often.

PRACTICE

TAKE TEN BALLS OR ORANGES AND TRY TO KEEP ALL OF THEM IN THE AIR.
HARD, RIGHT?

HAVE THINGS YOU BUY FOR YOURSELF GIFT-WRAPPED.

**GET A SHEET OF PAPER
AND DRAW NAKED BREASTS ALL OVER IT.
LARGE BREASTS. EVEN LARGER BREASTS.**

# YOU DESERVE SOME NEW CLOTHES.

Don't just wear them when your child is in bed.

WEAR HIGH HEELS FOR A WHILE,
AND THEN KICK THEM OFF.

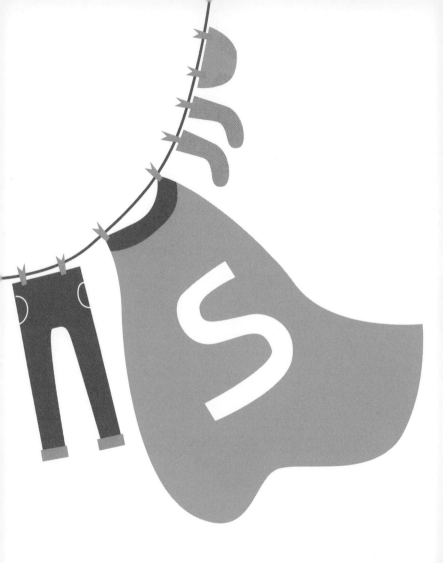

**TAKE OFF YOUR SUPERMOM CAPE.**

## NEVER MIND THE DISHES.
## FORGET THE GROCERIES. HUG!

Hugging and eye contact increase the level of oxytocin in your brain. Oxytocin makes you feel happy, so you'll hug even more and eventually become a hugaholic.

# YOU'RE DOING GREAT (AND MAKING IT LOOK GOOD).

Sing along at the top of your lungs, especially the "Mama" part.

# BRING THE PARTY HOME.

If you can't go to the party, the party will have to come to you.
Invite friends over. Give dinner parties. Drink at home.

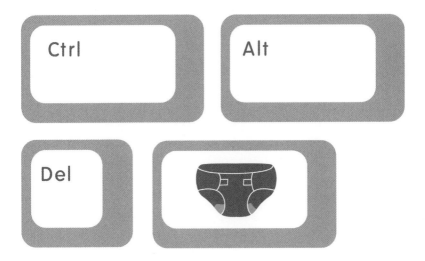

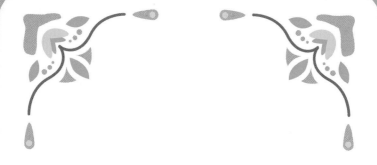

*Laugh so hard,*
*tears run down*
*your leg.*

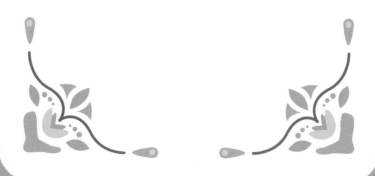

# DON'T FORGET YOURSELF.

1

2

6

**ME, MYSELF, AND I**

3

5

4

WRITE DOWN SIX THINGS YOU'VE DONE THIS WEEK
JUST FOR YOURSELF.

# PSYCHO TEST #1

## CHECK ALL THAT APPLY.

- YOU HATE A MESS.

- YOUR HOUSE IS A MESS.

- YOU CAN'T REMEMBER ANYTHING.

- YOU DON'T CARE ABOUT DEVELOPMENTAL STAGES OTHER THAN YOUR BABY'S CURRENT ONE.

- YOUR FINGERS SMELL FAINTLY OF POOP.

- YOU EAT BABY FOOD—AND LIKE IT.

- YOU HAVEN'T SHAVED YOUR LEGS IN TWO WEEKS.

- YOU SWAY LIKE YOU'RE HOLDING THE BABY—WHEN YOU'RE NOT HOLDING THE BABY.

- THE EVENING NEWS UPSETS YOU.

5 OR MORE OF THE 9 SYMPTOMS? DIAGNOSIS:
ADMD (ATTENTION-DEFICIT MOMMY DISORDER)

# PSYCHO TEST #2

- ☐ ON WALKS, YOU ARE PREPARED TO FIGHT OFF DOGS.
- ☐ YOU SCREAM WHEN A CHILD FALLS.
- ☐ YOU YELL THINGS LIKE, "NOW I'VE HAD IT!"
- ☐ YOU SING BABY SONGS IN PUBLIC.
- ☐ YOU WASH YOUR HANDS A LOT.
- ☐ YOU WALK REALLY FAST.
- ☐ YOU COMPLAIN ABOUT YOUR PARTNER.
- ☐ YOU HAVE NO PATIENCE AT THE CASH REGISTER.
- ☐ ALL YOUR PICTURES ARE OF THE BABY AND HIS DAD, BECAUSE YOU COMPULSIVELY TAKE ALL THE PICTURES.

## 5 OR MORE OF THESE 9 SYMPTOMS? DIAGNOSIS:
### MOMMY TOURETTE'S

YES, THEY'RE COMPLETELY NATURAL.

# ALWAYS BEING INCONSISTENT IS CONSISTENT, TOO.

# 5

*Stuff to help mommy and daddy*

# GO BUNGEE-JUMPING TOGETHER

Or do something else that's really corny. Spending time together without the kid is even more effective if you're doing something that's completely ridiculous.

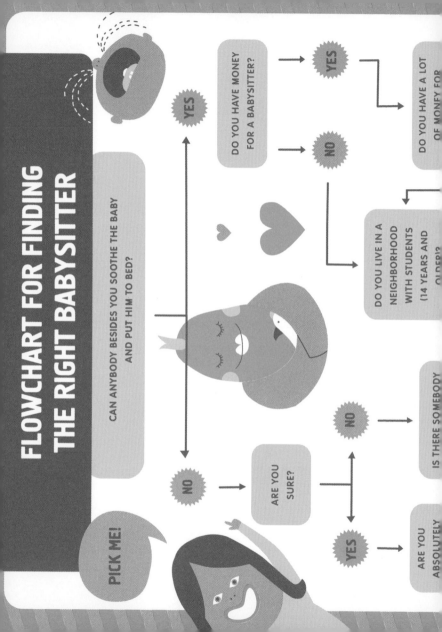

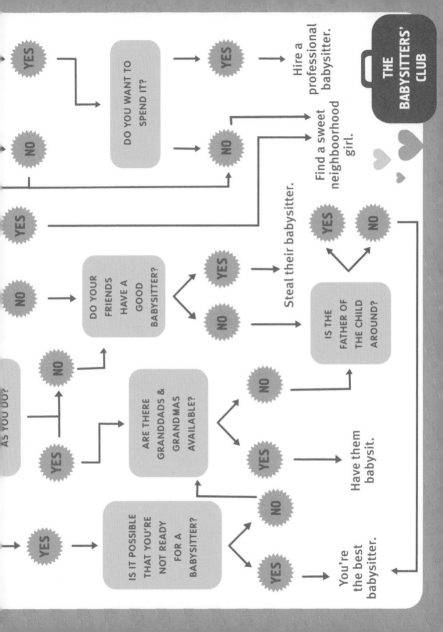

THE BABYSITTERS' CLUB

YES

DO YOU WANT TO SPEND IT? → YES → Hire a professional babysitter.

NO → NO

YES

AS YOU DO?

NO → DO YOUR FRIENDS HAVE A GOOD BABYSITTER? → YES → Steal their babysitter.

NO → IS THE FATHER OF THE CHILD AROUND? → YES / NO

YES

Find a sweet neighboorhood girl.

YES → ARE THERE GRANDDADS & GRANDMAS AVAILABLE? → NO → IS THE FATHER OF THE CHILD AROUND?

NO → YES → Have them babysit.

YES → IS IT POSSIBLE THAT YOU'RE NOT READY FOR A BABYSITTER? → NO

YES → You're the best babysitter.

## SAY SOMETHING WEIRD.

When you're stressed or having an argument with your partner, you tend to react in the same way, using the same patterns. Try not to do that for once. Say something that's unexpected.

THERE ARE PLENTY OF THINGS BESIDES SEX THAT YOU CAN DO IN BED, ON THE COUNTER, OR ON TOP OF A WORKING WASHING MACHINE.

**EXPLAIN CAREFULLY THAT A POT BELLY IS NOT SEXY.**

20 LBS.

In general, men gain over twelve pounds during their partner's pregnancy.

# BABY SLEEPING POSITIONS

THE CRITIC

THE OCTOPUS

THE CHERUB

THE GINGERBREAD MAN

STOP BEATING YOURSELF UP.

**COUCH-SLOUCHING IS THE NEW DATE NIGHT.**

# WORKSHOP #2:
## COMMUNICATING WITH YOUR PARTNER

MEN ARE IMMUNE TO SUBTLE HINTS, AND TYPICALLY RESPOND BEST TO DIRECT COMMUNICATION. HERE'S HOW TO EXPLAIN WHAT YOU WANT.

**1** Decide what you want.

**2** Begin your request with "Would you . . ."

**3** Provide a time frame if possible.

| YOUR DESIRE | REQUEST |
|---|---|
| To be sexy | "Would you like to have sex now?" |
| To have him stop doing that | "Would you please stop doing that as soon as possible?" |
| ............................... | ............................... |
| ............................... | ............................... |
| ............................... | ............................... |

# TOMORROW IS A NEW DAY.

CHERISH GRANDPAS, GRANDMAS, UNCLES, AND AUNTS—OR ADOPT A FEW.

# ISN'T IT HARD
# NOT TO TALK ABOUT YOUR KID?

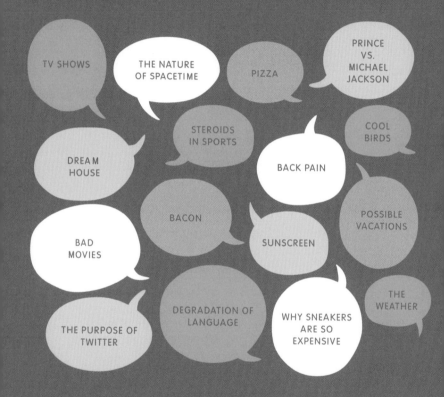

Keep these easy conversational subjects on hand.

**OPEN A BOTTLE OF CHAMPAGNE EVERY THREE MONTHS (OR MORE OFTEN).**

Congratulations!
You've survived another 100 days as mother and father.

"Good enough" is just great.

# PICK-ME-UP POSTCARDS

The following pages are postcards you can send to girlfriends who are in the same boat.

Feeling creative? Cut the cards from the back and front flaps of the book, write in your own messages, and make a friend happy.

YOU'RE A SUPERMOM.

www.knockknockstuff.com

# GIVE IN.

Let it all hang out.

KK

GRAB A BEER AND HIT THE DANCE FLOOR!

You've got more booty to shake!

www.knockknockstuff.com

KK